CATHARINE INGRAM
IT'S IN YOU!

GREATNESS

THE WORLD IS WAITING

Copyright © 2020 Catharine Ingram.

All rights reserved. No part of this publication may be reproduced, distributed, or transmitted in any form or by any means, including photocopying, recording, or other electronic or mechanical methods, without the prior written permission of the publisher, except in the case of brief quotations embodied in critical reviews and certain other noncommercial uses permitted by copyright law. For permission requests, write to the publisher, addressed "Attention: Permissions Coordinator," at the address below.

IT'S IN YOU!

Catharine Ingram
catharineingram@yahoo.com

ISBN 978-1-949027-69-3

Copyright © 2020

Published by
Destined To Publish | www.DestinedToPublish.com | 773.783.2981

DEDICATION

This book is dedicated to my granddaughter Marchaun, who has been endowed with more gifts than I could possibly dream of having. I challenge her to take advantage of the age in which she lives, when knowledge is at her fingertips, and to let nothing stand in the way of fulfilling her God-given purpose.

My prayer is that she learns early the lesson that took me years to learn: that our only limitations are self-imposed ones.

ACKNOWLEDGMENT

I want to thank my husband Thomas, my son Michael, and my daughter Michelle, who support every endeavor I undertake. And for their help on those days when I had writer's block, I want to thank three of my buddies who kept pushing me toward the finish line: Josephine Boyd, Barbara Thomas, and Lillie Foxx.

 # Contents

CHAPTER 1 1

CHAPTER 2 18

CHAPTER 3 35

CHAPTER 4 66

EPILOGUE 75

# Chapter 1

"What have I gotten myself into?" she wondered as she hobbled out of the airport terminal, recalling the last weekend she had spent with her granddaughter Bridgette and great-grandson Kevin. It had been three years earlier at their annual family reunion. That wonderful weekend, she'd seen new faces along with familiar ones. Everyone laughed and had a great time, all except Kevin. The entire weekend he was either on his tablet or his phone, or whining about being bored. All the other children were busy playing games, getting to know each other, setting up the tables, or doing whatever was needed.

"The last thing I need at my age is to be stuck for two weeks with a lazy eleven-year-old," she murmured as she set her purse on the seat and looked at her watch.

William came up behind her, carrying her tote full of books. "Wow, this is heavy. Are you going to read all of these books?" he asked.

"Absolutely."

He set her tote beside the seat and gave her a big hug. The talkative eight-year-old self-proclaimed expert at flying had made the flight enjoyable. He had told knock-knock jokes and talked about his classmates, his teachers, and his dog MJ, which loved to play catch. His mom was very quiet, not that she could get a word in edgewise.

"Keep up the good work. I am glad to have met you, William. Take good care of your mom," she added.

"You bet," he said as he grabbed his mom's luggage and waved goodbye. His mom waved also.

Mrs. Bee, a tall, stout elderly woman in her late eighties with thick, curly, silvery hair pulled back into a neat bun, waved goodbye, looked at her watch for the third time, adjusted the band, folded her shawl over her arm, and sat down. This had been her first time flying, and with the exception of the turbulence, it had been most enjoyable, thanks in part to William, who often traveled between his mom in Chicago and his dad in Memphis. He assured her that most of the time, the flights were smooth. She had a window seat and was amazed at how tiny everything looked on the ground. Taking advantage of a break from William as he ate his snacks, she'd gotten a little shuteye. Then she'd awakened to the most angelic view: fluffy, pure white clouds, a scene that made her think of what Heaven must look like.

Bee had not been to Chicago since her daughter Karen, Bridgette's mom, had passed ten years earlier. But when her granddaughter called, she was willing to help. At the last minute, Bridgette had to replace one of her coworkers on a trip to Arizona as they opened a new store. She would be gone for two weeks. Although they often called each other, Bee had not seen her granddaughter and great-grandson in years, so she decided to come a couple of days early just to spend time with them both before Bridgette would have to leave.

Grandma Bee checked the time and pulled a copy of Long Walk to Freedom from her tote. A car honked, and she looked up and waved as Bridgette pulled up to the curb. Bridgette exited the car and popped the trunk, expecting Kevin to grab his great-grandma's bag, but he was busy on his phone.

"Hi, Grandma!" shouted Bridgette. She gave Grandma Bee a warm hug, then grabbed her luggage and threw it in the trunk. "How was your flight?" she asked as she walked around to the driver's side.

"Better than I thought. It's so good to see you all. I see you are finally getting some meat on your bones," Grandma Bee said as she opened the passenger door.

"A little too much, I'm afraid," Bridgette complained as she put the key in the ignition.

"Well, you're as beautiful as ever. My, Kevin, how you've grown!" she said as she looked down at Kevin, who was in the passenger seat.

"Oh, sorry—hi, Grandma Bee." Kevin exited the car and got in the backseat, his face glued to his phone.

His mom shook her head in disbelief, then turned to Grandma Bee, who sat down and fastened her seatbelt. "If you aren't too tired, I'd like to stop at the grocery store for a minute to pick up a case of water and some snacks for you guys."

"I'm fine. I'd like to get some prune juice also."

"You're still drinking your juice, huh?"

Grandma Bee smiled. "Keep living, child. Keep living."

The store wasn't crowded. They were in and out in a jiffy. Grandma Bee couldn't help but take note of how Bridgette placed both bags and the two cases of water in the trunk while Kevin crawled into the backseat, eating his chips and playing on his phone. It took everything in her to hold her peace, but she knew today wasn't the time. After all, she hadn't even made it to their home yet.

The next few days were magical as they reminisced about old times. Grandma Bee was pleased to hear that the divorce had not made Bridgette bitter and that she and Kevin's dad, Rodney, were still friends. Bridgette confessed that although Rodney was not a great husband, he was a wonderful, dependable father. Unfortunately, two years earlier, his job had closed its main plant in Illinois and he had relocated to one of their facilities in Tennessee.

Grandma Bee and Bridgette baked cookies together that night like they had done numerous times when Bridgette was a teenager. They tried to get Kevin to join them, but he wasn't interested. He spent most of the time in his room, playing games. Several times his mom managed to coax him out only to notice later that he had returned. Bridgette had an early Sunday morning flight and would be returning in two weeks.

Grandma Bee stooped and looked beneath the saucepan as she adjusted the flames to a simmer before mopping up the splattered sauce from the stovetop. She was making her great-grandson's favorite; spaghetti and meatballs. She dipped out a spoonful and tasted it. Something was lacking! She rolled her eyes, thought for a moment, then added another dash of garlic powder and a pinch of crushed red pepper and tasted it again. This time she smiled, placed the spoon in the sink, and turned.

She watched Kevin twist, squirm, shuffle and groan at the kitchen table in front of her, clearly agitated. She asked, "Now, what's the problem?"

"It's too hard! My teacher wants us to read this chapter and write an essay. I don't—I don't know these big words. I don't know how to write no essay," he stammered, folded his arms, and slumped down in the chair. With his lip stuck out, he put his head down on the table.

Grandma Bee walked over to the table and picked up the sheet of paper in front of him. Other than his name, the paper was blank. With a look of disgust, she instructed him, "Raise your head up now. Never let me hear you say 'I can't' when you haven't even tried."

"But—"

"But nothing. But nothing! Your mom said you had two weeks to work on this assignment. I asked you twice if you needed help, and what did you say?"

He shrugged his shoulders.

"What did you say?" she questioned again.

"I thought—"

"Thought nothing. What did you say?"

"I said I didn't need any help," he murmured.

"Had you looked at the assignment?"

No answer.

"I asked you a question!" She elevated her voice.

"No," he whispered with his head down.

Clearly frustrated, she hesitated, choosing her words carefully. Looking at the blank page, she continued. "Young man, you have known about this assignment for two weeks. Your mom said you had a three-day weekend. There is absolutely no excuse for you to have not completed this assignment. The only thing I have seen you do is—" she made texting motions with her fingers, "—from the time you get up until the time you go to bed. I didn't say anything to your mom, but I heard you talking past eleven Friday night."

Kevin's eyes widened.

"Yes, old people may be in bed early, but it doesn't mean they are asleep, and the next time, I will tell your mom. Is that clear?"

He nodded his head with a sigh of relief.

"Child, all you have to do is get your lessons out," she reminded him. "You don't have any chores."

"What's chores?" he asked, perplexed.

"Chores . . . jobs . . . responsibilities."

"I do!" he insisted.

"What, other than fixing your bed?"

"I—a lot of stuff."

"Well, like what?"

"I clean my room."

Grandma Bee's head swiftly turned toward the hall. She took two steps backward to see into his bedroom. His Chicago Bears comforter was balled up on the bed. Several pieces of a puzzle were on the floor along with an empty juice box and an empty potato chip bag. She looked at him accusingly.

"I haven't finished cleaning it up today yet."

GREATNESS — IT'S IN YOU!

"Okay," she replied, ignoring the untidy room. "What else?"

"I can't think right now," he confessed.

"Your mom works really hard to provide you with the things you need as well as stuff you just want. Anything you want, she gets it for you. Nice clothes, toys, an allowance . . ." she shook her head, then continued. "Kevin, you're a bright young man. Your problem is you don't apply yourself."

He dropped his head.

"The only thing you get excited about is basketball. Now, there's nothing wrong with wanting to be a great NBA player, but even if you become a great player—"

"Oh, I am. I'm good! I'm really good, Grandma Bee!" With enthusiasm, he pushed back from the table and jumped up to score with an imaginary ball. "I'm going to be a millionaire one day. I'm going to be very successful. Buy my mom any house she wants," he bragged with a proud look on his face as he stared off into space.

"I know, I know. Your Uncle Milton talks about you all the time. He thinks you have potential, but that's all the more reason for you to do well in school. Without an education and with a bad manager, you'll go from a millionaire to a . . . to a dollar-aire in no time." The both laughed.

"Do you know what I wanted to be when I was your age?"

"What?" he asked curiously.

She pulled a chair out from the table and sat down. She was quiet for a moment. One could tell she was reliving her past. Her jaws flinched, but no words came forth. Kevin didn't know what to say, so he said nothing.

Finally, she spoke. "I wanted to be a nurse. You see, I grew up on a small farm in Mississippi and we had lots of chickens, turkeys, hogs. Oh, yeah, and we had two cows. Whenever one of the baby chicks or pigs got sick, I took care of them. I made sure they had a warm place to sleep and I got an old nipple and a baby bottle and fed them, nursing them back to health. One time, when one of our baby pigs got sick, I brought him in the house and fed him until he got well. Once he was feeling better, he would follow me around the house. He was like a pet."

"A big ole pig?"

"No, he wasn't that big," she chuckled.

"Did you give him a name?"

"Yep!"

He waited.

She was reliving the story.

"Grandma Bee, what you name him?"

"Piggy . . . I named him Piggy."

They both laughed.

She pushed back the chair and stood up. "I was really sad that Thanksgiving when hog-killing time came around."

"Why they had to kill him?"

"For food, child. For food."

"Y'all ate pig? Yuck!"

"Yes, that's where our meat came from: hogs, chicken, fish, and rabbits!"

"I wouldn't eat no pig and rabbits. Yuck. I would be a veterinarian," he announced.

"You mean vegetarian," she corrected.

"I sure wouldn't eat no fat, stinky pig."

She eyed him suspiciously. "Ah, what kind of sandwich did you take for lunch?"

"Ham and cheese."

"Uh-huh. That's what I thought." She nodded.

She continued. "One time my baby sister got sick with the mumps. You see, we didn't go to no doctor for every little thing. Why we never went to the doctor? Well, with the mumps—"

"What are mumps? Big bumps?"

"No, no, no. Children don't have mumps nowadays. Mumps were when your jaws would swell up really big like this." She held her hands out from the side of her face and, with a deep breath, puffed out her jaws. She was quiet for a moment. You could tell the memory was clear in her mind.

"I put sardine oil on her jaws and in about a week she was all better."

She continued. "Another time, Papa cut a deep gash in his leg on some barbed wire. It became infected. I had seen our neighbor Miss Ann take care of a cut, so I knew what to do. I cleaned the cut and poured some coal oil in it. It healed and barely left a scar. I also used to watch my grandma make dandelion tea when people had the flu. I loved helping people get well."

"So, you wanted to be a doctor?'

"Shucks, no, but I wanted to be a nurse. I dreamed about wearing one of those crisp white dresses. Dress as white as the clouds in the sky and that little white cap."

"Oh, I remember you wearing a white dress when we came to visit you one time."

She shook her head. "No, that was my church usher uniform."

Curiously, he asked, "Well, what kind of work did you do, Grandma Bee?"

"I did get to wear a white uniform, all right. I was a maid. Yes, that's right, I was a maid."

"A maid? For real?"

"Yes. You see, when I was twelve, Ma got real sick. Me being the oldest of the three, I had to drop out of school and help out. Times were hard and with no brother, well, I had to help PaPa in the field through the week. On the weekend I would go over Mrs. Frances' house and wash and iron her clothes. She didn't pay me much, but she always gave us the clothes her children outgrew, so that helped a lot. Ma was sick off and on for over three years. By the time she got well, I had missed so much and had grown so tall that I was embarrassed to go back with the smaller girls and boys. But you? You have so many opportunities. You can be anything you want to be!"

"Well, I know I ain't going to be no maid . . . do men be maids?"

"A man would be a butler."

"Well, I ain't going to be no butler, either. I'm going to be a famous basketball player like Kobe Bryant. I dream about it sometimes."

"I know you aren't. Times are much different now. You can be anything you want to be if you want it bad enough. And, yes, it's good to have dreams, but it takes more than dreams to be successful. Without hard work, that's all you're going to have—a dream. Come on, let me help you with that homework. Time is moving," she said, glancing at the clock on the microwave. "Read the first chapter."

"I can't read good."

"It's read well, and I told you to never say you can't! You can learn anything by repetition, repetition, repetition!"

"I don't know what repetition mean," he confessed.

"It means the same way you learn all those dance moves, rap songs, knock-knock jokes . . . and, yes, those basketball moves is the way you learn anything. You practice, practice, practice!"

"But—"

She hit the table with her fist. "But nothing! Do you have any idea how blessed you are, young man?" Not waiting for a reply, she continued. "I mean, do you? There are millions of kids who wish they had the opportunities you have. Even in 2020, there are kids in some countries who walk miles to school. Some don't even have shoes. You have several pairs of shoes and gym shoes."

"I have three pair of new gym shoes. I have six pairs in all. I even have a pair of Jordans," he bragged. "One boy in my class wears the same pair every day."

"It doesn't matter what's on your feet, but what's in your head," she reminded him.

"Huh?" he asked.

His phone rang. He reached for it, but she grabbed it first.

She looked at it and put it in her apron pocket. "Look, I was with your mom when she went shopping for your school clothes. Your clothes cost as much as hers." She shook her head. "I don't understand young parents these days."

"She wants me to be cool," he said, sitting up proudly in his chair.

Grandma Bee mumbled, "Great combination, dumb and cool."

"What?" he asked.

"Uh, how was school?"

"Good. Can I have a snack?"

"Yes, we have oranges and apples in the fridge."

"Can I have that ham sandwich now?"

She stopped and turned. "Didn't you have a ham sandwich in your lunch?"

He was silent.

"Well, didn't you?"

"Terry had this cool game—"

"What about your lunch?"

"I traded my lunch for this game." He proudly pulled a small toy from his pocket.

Without saying a word, she walked over to the fridge and pulled out an apple and an orange. "Which one?"

Understanding her fully, he answered, "The orange. Thanks, Grandma. You're the bestest grandma in the whole world!"

"Yeah, sure."

"Grandma Bee, can you—"

"Will you."

"Will I what?"

She turned and gave him that look.

"Oh, sorry. We're raising money for our basketball uniforms. Will you make me three dozen tea cakes for our bake sale tomorrow? The whole class and my teacher love your cookies."

"What about this? I'll give you the recipe and you make them. After all, some of the world's best chefs are men, you know."

"I know. I watch the cooking channel with Uncle Milton when I spend the weekend with them."

"Finish your snack and we'll get started."

"Thanks, Grandma Bee."

Grandma Bee pulled the measuring spoons from the drawer. She walked over to the pantry and set out the sugar and flour on the counter.

"Give me a piece of paper and a pen, please," instructed Grandma Bee as she sat down at the table.

Kevin gave her his pen and a sheet of paper. He stood over her shoulder as she wrote out the recipe.

Grandma Bee sensed a shift in his body language as she wrote. "Okay, what's wrong?"

"I can't read cursive."

"What grade are you?"

"Sixth."

She looked at him for a moment before turning the paper over and printing the recipe. "Turn the TV off in the living room, please."

"All right, Grandma Bee." He rushed out of the room.

"Grandma, I don't see the remote control."

"Boy, use your head!"

"Huh?"

"Boy, use your hands, boy. Use your hands."

He came back into the kitchen, looking sheepish. "I'm recording Jeopardy for you. It's coming on in a little while."

"Thanks. I didn't realize it was so late. Thanks, G-Son."

He smiled. "You haven't called me that in a long time."

"Well, you haven't called me in a long time, period."

"I be busy."

"Yeah, right." She passed him the pen and the recipe. "Remember, you're making three batches, so you have to multiply the recipe times three."

He looked at the recipe and his countenance dropped.

"Okay, what's wrong?"

"I know how to multiply, but I don't know how to multiply fractions. The only kids in the room that do fractions are the Asian kids."

She sat back in her chair. "We need to talk. Put the paper down. The cookies can wait." She stared at the table as she racked her brain, looking for the right words to challenge him yet not crush his spirit. After several minutes, as lovingly and as quietly as possible, she reminded him, "Kevin, this is your second year in the sixth grade."

"Miss Jenkins failed me for—"

"No, we are not playing the blame game. Miss Jenkins didn't fail you. You failed yourself." She found her voice rising and fought hard to control it. "Yes, she wrote the F, but it was you who earned it. Look, God made all people and He didn't make one smarter than the other. The Asian kids, the Chinese kids, the Russian kids, the Austrian kids—none are any smarter than you. Now, if they are making better grades, it's simply because while you're playing on your phone, they're studying. Kevin, how bad do you want to be an NBA basketball player?"

He came alive at once and started twisting and turning in the chair with excitement. In a flash, he was out of the chair, pretending to dribble and dunk. "Really bad. Really, really bad. More than anything in the whole wide world!"

"Well, anytime you want something so bad it causes you to—" she started wiggling and twisting, "—you're on the right trail for getting it." They both laughed.

"Let me tell you a story about a woman named Annie Mae who was born in Mississippi back in the late 1840s. Then we're going to have to get started on those cookies or your mama will have to pick some up from Jewels."

"No, my teacher wants yours. Everybody say yours are the best!"

Grandma Bee started laughing.

"What's funny, Grandma Bee?" he asked, looking bewildered.

"I was just thinking about the first time I made those cookies." She could barely talk, she was laughing so hard. "Your grandfather and I were courting. We had gotten in a big argument the day before. I realized I was wrong, but I was too stubborn to apologize, so I was going to make him some cookies instead. The recipe called for two spoonfuls of baking soda. Well, the only spoon I saw my mama stirring up the bread with was a big wooden spoon. Your grandpa came calling by the time I started making the cookies. He came into the kitchen by the time I added the baking soda. Boy, the batter started rising and bubbling up so much, your grandpa accused me of trying to poison him."

By now Grandma Bee was laughing so hard, tears were coming out of her eyes.

"Who taught you how to make them, then?"

Pulling herself together, she wiped her eyes. "Well, I just kept trying and trying until I got it right. Remember what I said? Repetition, repetition." Dabbing the apron to her eyes, she added, "Every weekend I would make them. Each time they got better and better. Why, I won two blue ribbons at our church picnic two years in a row. I beat out about a hundred other ladies in the church."

Kevin got up and went around the table. He held up her arm and in a grown-up voice he hollered out, "The undefeated cookie champion of the world—my grandma!"

"Come on, child. Let me finish telling you about Annie Mae."

# CHAPTER 2

It was a cold fall day right before harvest. In a small room, a young slave girl about eleven years old, wearing a flour-sack sleeveless dress, placed a hoecake in each of three tin pans. There were no utensils. She filled three tin cans with water. In the corner, two small boys were riding their stick horses. Their clothes were tattered and several sizes too small, their feet were dirty and bare, yet they were happy. They had each other.

The wooden floor was bare, burlap sacks instead of drapes hung from the small window, and light shined through a small hole in the roof. In one corner was a pallet with corn shucks poking out one of the seams. It was covered with a quilt made from scraps.

"Did y'all hear me? Get over here and eat your sum'teet fo' it get cold."

Before he even reached his pan, Sam hollered out, "I want some more milk on my bread! I ain't got but a little. Little Henry got more than me."

"No, I ain't!"

"Yeah, you do!"

Milk was scarce. Annie Mae opened her mouth to say something, then stopped. "Okay." She got up, took the pan, walked over to the table, and pretended to pour. She placed the pan down in front of him. "This is all you get."

He smiled at his brother victoriously.

"I want some mo'," announced Little Henry.

"You ain't eat what you got. Your eyes bigger than your belly," she said as she tickled his stomach. They all laughed.

"Do me, do me!" begged Sam.

"Eat your sum'teet fo' it get cold."

Annie Mae took the iron and poked the coals in the fireplace, uncovering several small sweet potatoes. She placed them on the table and brushed off the ashes. They would be for dinner the next day.

"Annie Mae, bring me some water," her mom whispered from the bedroom.

"Coming, Ma." She jumped up, grabbed a tin can from the wall rack, filled it with water from a tin bucket, and carried it in the direction of the voice.

The room was dark and eerie as the shadows of the lamp's flames cast wavy lines on the wall near the bed. The heavy burlap makeshift curtains were drawn. The room reeked of sickness. Annie Mae would have to change the sheets. The covers rose and fell and the wheezing grew increasingly louder as her mother struggled with each breath. Annie Mae prayed and hoped the fear in her heart would not betray the forced smile on her face.

She rushed to the bed as her mom fought to sit up. Large beads of sweat slowly trickled down Ma's forehead, over the dried tears at the corner of her eyes, and through the snot trailing from her nose, settling on her parched lips.

Ma had been in bed for three days.

Annie Mae held the cup and her hands trembled with fear as her mom gulped the water.

"Thank you," Ma whispered as she slowly lowered her head to the damp pillow. The fever had returned. Annie Mae brushed the wet hair back from Ma's face. Ma looked much older than thirty with the heavy bags under her eyes from a lack of sleep, parched lips from the fever, and dry skin that looked like leather.

"How ya brothers, child? Are they okay?"

"Yes, ma'am."

Her mom forced a smile and touched Annie Mae's face. "I thank the good Lord every day for giving me a sweet child like you," she confessed before breaking out in a coughing spell. Mucus ran down her chin. Annie Mae wiped it up as her mom slowly laid her head on the pillow.

Her mom pulled the covers up beneath her chin and closed her eyes. Annie Mae watched, feeling helpless, then dipped her fingers in the tin can and rubbed her mom's forehead several times. As Ma drifted off to sleep, snoring softly, Annie Mae quietly tiptoed toward the door. The wooden floor squeaked loudly and she froze, then turned toward the bed. Her mom was undisturbed.

As Annie Mae quietly closed the door, Mrs. Henderson, a dumpy, obese white woman with her long blonde hair piled up on her head, burst through the front door with her tall, skinny daughter Emma Jo towering over her. They frightened Annie Mae's brothers, who ran to her, one on each side of her legs. They always burst in unannounced and always left the door opened when they left.

"Annie Mae, I need you to come up to the house this evening and make three batches of teacakes. The mayor and his wife, Mr. and Mrs. Clemmons, are coming for dinner this evening and we have nothing sweet to offer them. You will have to sleep over on the back porch because ain't no telling what time those greedy folks gonna leave, I tell you."

"Mama is kind of ailing and Pa ain't gotten back from picking up the supplies over in Spring Town. Ain't nobody to tend to the young'uns."

Mrs. Henderson looked over her glasses in amazement. "Annie, I ain't asking you. I'm telling you what you gon' do. Understand me?"

Annie Mae dropped her head. "Yes'm."

Mrs. Henderson looked down at the boys holding on to Annie Mae's legs. "How old are they?"

Patting the back of the one on her left leg, Annie Mae answered, "Sam here is six and Little Henry here is four and a half, ma'am."

Mrs. Henderson snorted. "They can keep themselves for one night."

Emma Jo, her nose in the air with a look of disgust, jumped back as Little Henry touched her bright red parasol.

Little Henry was frightened as she yelled, "Keep your filthy little hands off my things!" and brushed off imaginary crumbs. He hid behind Annie Mae, who patted his back to comfort him.

"Annie Mae, you better teach that young'un some manners."

"He didn't mean no harm. He just like bright colors and shiny things."

"Either you teach 'em, or I will!"

Annie Mae knew very well what that meant.

Emma Jo spotted a beautiful royal blue velvet dress hanging from a stick placed over two nails on the wall. She rushed over and her eyes widened as she caressed the soft fabric, watching the colors go from dark to light.

"Ma, look! Look, Ma! Annie Mae stole this dress from someone."

"That's Annie Mae's dress!" Little Henry stepped forward and proclaimed.

Emma Jo shot him an evil look that caused him to recoil and hide behind his sister.

Annie Mae wrapped her arm protectively around her brother and patted his back while insisting, "I did no such thing."

"Watch your mouth, girlie. Don't you go there calling my child a liar, you hear? Now, where you get this dress from?"

"I made it!"

"Don't lie to me. You know what happens when you lie to me."

"Yes, ma'am," said Annie Mae, remembering the beating she got the last time, when Emma Jo broke an expensive vase and blamed her. "I ain't lying. Mrs. Patterson gave me some curtains she didn't want and I made this dress with my own two hands. I sew a little every night after I put my brothers to bed."

"She's lying, Ma. She's lying. Why, Ma, you can't even sew that good. I bet she stole it from Mrs. Butler when you sent her down there for to help when she was sick."

Shaking her head, Mrs. Henderson disagreed. "No, it sure ain't one of that highfalutin' woman's dresses. Why, she can't get half of her big behind in this dress."

"Can I have it, Ma? Can I?" Emma Jo pleaded as she twirled around, holding the dress to her chest.

"Well, it does look like it fits you perfect and that color goes nicely with your blonde hair. The Fall Ball is in two weeks and we haven't had a chance to go to town and pick you out a dress."

"Yes, you can. Now we just have to find something for your sister to wear."

Emma Jo squealed with delight. "Wait until I show Lillie my beautiful dress!" She rushed out the door.

"Don't forget to be at the house before the sun goes down," Mrs. Henderson ordered Annie Mae before exiting, once again leaving the door wide open.

"Don't cry, Annie Mae. Why, the devil gonna get mean old Mrs. Henderson with her ugly self," announced Sam.

Annie Mae tried not to laugh but she couldn't help thinking that was the way she would describe Mrs. Henderson, whose skin color was somewhere between gold and orange with brown spots all over. Her height and width were about the same. She had a long nose with a hump and a mole resting on the bridge of it. Her hair was the color of gold and so thin her scalp showed in places.

"It's not nice to say those things, Sam."

"Well, she is. Ain't she, Little Henry?"

His brother nodded his head vigorously.

"Come on. Let me tuck you all in bed," she said sorrowfully, glancing at the empty wall. The only nice dress she'd ever had. It just wasn't right, she thought. Every day while feeding the chickens and milking the cows, she would see Emma Jo and her sister Lillie on their way to school, wearing beautiful dresses and with beautiful ribbons in their hair. It just wasn't fair. They had many dresses. She'd only had one, and now she had none.

Two days later, Annie Mae was coming out of the chicken coop with a basket full of eggs. "I have to be careful. I have to be careful," she whispered over and over, taking very small steps. She didn't notice Emma Jo and Lillie tiptoeing up behind her.

Giggling, Emma Jo placed her finger to her lip and motioned for Lillie to be silent. "Boo!"

The basket fell to the ground. Annie Mae stared in horror as the cracked eggs ran out of the woven basket, forming a puddle in the grass. Quickly, she regained her composure and began picking them up. Fortunately, only three of the nineteen eggs were broken.

Standing over Annie Mae, Emma Jo threatened her. "Oooooooh, look what you did! We gonna tell mom you were playing with the eggs. Right, Lillie?"

Lillie looked confused. "We scared her, Emma Jo."

Emma Jo was two years older than Lillie and meaner than a hound dog. She gave Lillie a stern look and insisted, "You saw her playing with the eggs. She was juggling them, right?"

"I didn't—"

Emma Jo moved closer to Lillie. "You saw her, right?"

Lillie's face changed to a look of defeat. "Yes, I saw her playing with the eggs."

Annie Mae could see where this was going. "It was an accident!"

Emma Jo reminded Annie Mae, "Ma don't like it when you call us liars. Remember what happened the last time?"

Annie Mae nodded with her head down.

Emma Jo put on a vile smirk. "Now, I was just thinking to myself this morning: Sometimes Ma act like we are slaves, having us make our own beds and iron our clothes. I mean, why should we have to do anything except be beautiful? Now, you look-a here. Look at me when I'm talking to you, girlie."

Annie Mae lifted her head and found it almost impossible to suppress a laugh as she looked into Emma Jo's face. With the exception of the mole, she was her mother's twin. As she stared at Emma Jo, a lot of words came to her mind to describe her, but beautiful was not one of them.

"Now, the way I see it, you owe us. We won't tell Mama if you do our chores the whole month."

"But—"

"Say it! Say it! You were playing with the eggs," she demanded.

Annie Mae swallowed hard. "I was playing with the eggs."

"Good," said Emma Jo, satisfied. "Now, this is the plan. You have to do them on Saturday when Ma and Pa go into town. You have to wash and iron our clothes and clean up our room for the whole month or we gonna tell. You hear?"

Annie Mae nodded her head as Emma Jo tossed her hair and walked off arrogantly.

Just as Lillie was about to say something, Emma Jo shouted, "Let's go, Lillie!" With a sad look, Lillie turned and ran to catch up with her sister.

A month later, after Annie had finished both her own chores and the Henderson girls', she slipped off into the woods. She constantly checked over her shoulders to make sure she wasn't followed. She hated lying to her Ma and Pa, but she couldn't tell them what she was about to do. The sound of cracking twigs beneath her feet was amplified with each step she took. Her back and chest hurt from carrying the heavy buckets of water for drinking, washing dishes, and bathing from the pump to the big house every evening. She wasn't sure if she was hearing her heart pounding or her mind playing tricks on her. Her feet became tangled in vines and pulled her to the ground, into a cocklebur patch. She scrambled to her knees and froze as she heard the rustling of the bushes and a sharp object poked into her back. Fear paralyzed her until she realized she had backed into a broken tree limb.

Dirty, salty sweat ran down her forehead and across her lip. Covered in cockleburs, she knew exactly what would happen if someone found out. She flinched at the thought of the whip on her naked back, yet the thought of being able to read gave her the strength and courage to keep going.

Her eyes scanned the woods for any sign of movement. A sigh of relief filled her heart when a small jackrabbit hopped from under the brush and scurried away.

"Chirp. Chirp. Chirp. Hoot." That was the signal, three chirps and one hoot.

"Miss Jones?" whispered Annie Mae as she turned around and around in great expectation.

To her surprise, a young white girl who looked about her age stepped out from behind an oak tree. She was dressed in men's clothes with a heavy blanket draped over her shoulders.

"Are you—"

"Yes, I'm Bessie Jones. You look surprised."

"I was expecting—"

"Someone older," Bessie finished her sentence. "Are you sure you weren't followed?"

"I'm sure. I zigzagged all over the woods. No one could have kept up with me."

"Here, sit down. You're shaking like a leaf."

Annie Mae sat down and crossed her legs Indian style. She wasn't sure why she was shaking. It could have been because of the chill in the air. It could have been because she knew the consequences of getting caught. Or it could have been the excitement of knowing that she was finally getting the chance to learn how to read and write.

"Ain't no need of 'tending. I ain't scared cause I is, but I'm mo' scared of the kind of life I'll have if I don't learn how to read and write. I just gotta learn how. I just gotta. They told me you would help me. Will you? Will you please?" She pulled a coin from her pocket. "This all I got. Mrs. Greenberry paid me for helping her last summer. I've been saving it all this time." She extended it to Miss Jones.

"That's yours. Put it away. We don't have much time, only a few hours before dark. I can only help you one day of the week. I don't have to tell you what will happen to you if you get caught, but what you don't know is my punishment will be almost as bad."

Annie Mae was shocked to hear that. She had heard about slaves being beaten until their backs were raw or getting their thumbs cut off. She even knew of men being sold and separated from their families for trying to learn how to read, but never of white folks being beaten or punished.

"If they knew I was helping you, no one would do business with my family. None of the white children would talk to me. They wouldn't sell my parents anything at the hardware store."

"Why you—"

"Why I do it? Cause it's the right thing to do. None of us have the right to own people. We are all the same, just the outside is different sometimes. Why, my sister's hair is brown, mines is blonde, and my grandmother's is black as coal. But knowing what they will do to you if they find out, what makes you take the risk?"

"One day we were all in the field picking cotton, a whole lot of us. Evening come, we were heading to our shacks and we looked up to see a bunch of white men with Mr. Henderson. Sumthin' told us it wasn't good. Mr. Henderson walked up to a man named Boe and told him that he heard he was teaching some of us to read. He said Boe was a troublemaker and we didn't need to know how to read cause we had food an' a place to rest our head. He told Boe to tell everybody that they didn't need to know how to read. He said to say it out loud.

"I was hoping Boe would just say it, but he wouldn't. Why, Boe went on to say that a man ain't half a man if he can't read and write. That made them even madder. I was so scared, my mouth was as dry as the ground I stood on. My chest felt like it was about to burst open. I was hoping he would just say it even if he didn't mean it, just say it so they would go away, but he wouldn't. Why, they was ready to string Boe up right there, but Mr. Henderson stopped them. He said something real low—we couldn't make it out—and they left.

"The next day, Boe was gone. Nobody know what happened for sure, but we gotta pretty good idea. I made up my mind that day that education must be 'portant if people try so hard to keep you from it. I made up my mind somehow I was going to get me one."

"Well, it's getting late. Let's go. It isn't safe here. There is a pit in the ground a little ways from here. We keep it covered with brush. That's where we'll study. Come, I'll show you."

The next summer, while the other slaves were in the field, Mr. and Mrs. Henderson were in town for supplies, and their daughters were horseback riding with friends, this was the perfect time for Annie Mae to study her spelling words and her numbers. With a big dishpan of crowder peas in her lap and a small pail at her side for the hulls, Annie Mae sat Indian style on the kitchen floor as she shelled. Her spelling words were written on the front of a torn piece of paper, and scribbled on the back were some addition problems. The paper was propped against the pail.

A loose plank creaked in the floor behind her and she froze as fear gripped her heart. Slowly she tried to cover the paper with the tail of her dress, but it was too late. Emma Jo walked in front of her with a look of victory on her face. Annie Mae's heart pounded and her hands trembled.

Without saying a word, Emma Jo walked over and snatched the pail, exposing the piece of paper. Lillie picked it up and attempted to read it.

"I'm gonna tell PaPa that you're trying to learn how to read like white folks. Wait until he finds out."

Annie Mae was frozen in fear and couldn't say a word.

"You think because you can cook and sew and stuff, you're as good as us. You're not!"

"I can't read. I was just looking at the paper."

"We heard you, didn't we, Lillie? Didn't we?"

Lillie nodded, looking over her sister's shoulder. "She can read big words, Emma. Look," she directed as she pointed to the words. "Emma, she can help us pass to the next grade. I don't want to be in the same grade another year. We're the biggest children in the class already."

"We don't need the likes of her to help us."

"But she knows big words," Lillie reminded her as she turned the paper over. "Look, she can add big numbers, too."

Emma Jo's mouth dropped. "I bet the answers are wrong."

"Let's ask the teacher tomorrow and if they are right, she can teach us," Lillie pleaded.

"They better be right," Emma Jo warned before turning on her heels and heading for the door.

"She is real smart," noted Lillie.

"She ain't smart. Anyone can read those words."

"We can't."

"Shut up, Lillie."

Three months later, Emma Jo sauntered into the kitchen with a smirk on her face. She was eating rock candy "Papa says we can have anything we want for dinner tonight because we got all A's and two B's. He said you have to fix it. Papa is so proud of our hard work! So, I want blueberry pie, fried chicken, green beans, and cornbread. Tell her what you want, Lillie."

Lillie looked sad. "I'll eat the same as you."

"You don't have to. Papa said we can have anything we want."

Lillie whispered to Emma Jo, "Ain't we gonna say thank you?"

"For what?" she asked, not understanding. "That's her job, to help us with anything," she added as she hurried out the door. "And hurry up. Mama is going to fix our hair."

"Shucks! Annie Mae, you can be a real teacher. I didn't understand the way the teacher taught us to do 'rithmetic, but I understood the way you explained it. I—I just want to say I'm much obliged. Why, Emma Jo and me ain't never got no A or B on our test."

Annie Mae didn't say a word.

CATHARINE INGRAM

"Well, I just had to show my 'preciation somehow, so I saved this candy PaPa gave us yesterday." She handed Annie Mae something folded up in a crisp white handkerchief embroidered with tiny purple flowers.

She stopped at the door and turned. "I'm glad you learned how to read," she said before hurrying to catch up with her sister.

Annie waited until she heard the front door close before she unwrapped the handkerchief. Five pieces of cinnamon rock candy. Her favorite! She smiled and looked toward the door. "You're welcome."

Later one Friday evening, Annie Mae was on her knees, polishing the hardwood floor in the foyer, when Mrs. Henderson walked in with Mrs. Butler.

"I'm sorry, Annie Mae," said Mrs. Butler. "Don't mean to walk on your freshly polished floor."

Mrs. Henderson scowled. "Nonsense. It's no problem. That child can go back over it."

Mrs. Butler looked as though she wanted to say something, but Mrs. Henderson steered her toward the parlor.

Annie Mae picked up her bucket to start over at the front door. As she was about to set the bucket down, she overheard Mrs. Butler mention Bessie's name. She dropped the bucket and the polish ran down the hallway.

"Annie Mae, you better not break anything in there. You hear me?"

"No ma'am, I ain't broke nothin'," said Annie Mae, remembering the beating she had gotten two weeks earlier.

Rushing to meet her friends, Emma Jo had run down the stairs and bumped into the table in the foyer. Mrs. Henderson's expensive vase had broken. Emma Jo had denied breaking it and accused Annie Mae, and Mrs. Henderson had believed her daughter.

Annie Mae hurriedly mopped up the polish. She'd planned to do the dining area next, but after overhearing the conversation, she decided to polish the guest room, which was across the hall from the parlor.

"Yes, they caught Bessie Jones Friday evening, out in the woods teaching a couple of slaves how to read. One of the slaves over on the Robersons' plantation had noticed a couple of the young men going in the woods, so he followed them. When he saw her teaching, he went back and told Mr. Roberson. He said she was helping a young slave girl, too, but her back was turned and he didn't get a good look at her. He said he might be able to recognize her by her head."

"I knew that child was trouble with all of her New York ideas. Ever since she started spending the summer up north, she's changed," confessed Mrs. Henderson.

"Well, the city council had a secret meeting and told her grandmother that if the child stayed in town, no one would do business with her. No one would buy from her or sell to her. They say someone broke in their home Sunday while they were at church and burned up all of her books in the front yard. They say she had hundreds of books. Dolly Mae's husband, who works at the general store, said he saw the grandmother putting her on the noon train."

Annie Mae prayed. "Lord, it's me again. Don't mean to worry you, but please let Bessie be okay. She ain't like the rest *of them. She try to help people. Lord, please help her, and Lord, thank you for sending her my way so she can teach me how to read. If she can risk her life helping poor little old me, I know I can risk my life helping my own, and that's what I'm gon' do. That's all I want to say."*

Chapter 3

"What happened to Annie Mae?" Kevin asked.

"Well, Mr. Henderson died about two months later. The very next year, Mrs. Henderson married some rich man from Virginia who didn't believe in slavery. She and Emma Jo moved back to Virginia with him. Lillie never got married, but she treated the slaves pretty good. She never forgot how Annie Mae always helped her and her sister with their homework. When Annie Mae turned twenty-one, Lillie wrote her out a freedom bill. Annie Mae moved to Philadelphia and a Quaker woman who owned a restaurant hired her to be the head cook. People came from miles and miles around just to eat her cooking. Yes, she was some kind of cook. I still remember going over Grandma Ann's house for Sunday dinners."

Kevin's mouth was wide open. "You mean Annie Mae was your—"

"Yes. Yes, she was. She was my great-great-grandmama. I remember grown people coming over to her house after church. Yes, even when she was in her early eighties and her sight was getting dim, she was still helping people learn how to read. She would repeat something Frederick Douglass said: 'To deny education to any person is one of the greatest crimes against the human race.'"

With his elbow resting on the table, Kevin sat still, biting his fingernail. He pondered what she had just told him. "I would have learned how to read and write. I wouldn't have cared what those honkies said. Nobody would've stopped me!" he announced.

"Boy, shut your mouth! You don't know what you're talking—"

"But Grandma Bee, it wasn't fair that—"

"Of course it wasn't fair. Life isn't fair, but you have to learn to play the hand you're dealt. How are you so sure you would have been determined to learn how to read with all of the opposition they had then, when—" She treaded lightly, but kept pushing forward, "—when you can barely read with absolutely no opposition now?"

Embarrassed, feeling guilty, Kevin stared at the table.

"And don't ever let me hear you call anyone a honky or a nigger! To call them that is to lower yourself to their level. One thing you never, ever want to do is allow them to get you to stoop to their low level. I never want you to call your brother or sister the N-word! Don't allow anyone, black or white, to get you to see or talk about your own as though they are inferior or a low-life. You hear me?"

Kevin nodded his head.

"And you don't know what you would do. None of us knows what we will do under the right circumstances. None of us. So be careful about saying what you would or wouldn't do. Just pray to the good Lord that you're never put to the test."

He nodded. He knew what she was saying. "I understand, Grandma. One time—"

Seeing his face, she encouraged him. "Go on."

Remorsefully, he admitted, "One time I saw Mrs. Watts, the cafeteria lady, drop a dollar in the hallway. I started to keep it, but I didn't."

Grandma Bee smiled. "We have all been tempted."

"You, Grandma Bee?"

She nodded.

"No way!"

"Yes way!"

He sat up straight. "Tell me, Grandma," he pleaded.

She eyed him skeptically. "Okay, I will.

"When I was young, Ma and PaPa would give us Saturday money, what you would call your weekly allowance. They would take us with them uptown on Saturday evening when they went grocery shopping. One time when I was about ten, I decided to steal a bottle of fingernail polish. I had money in my pocket, but I was going to take it anyway. As soon as I dropped it in my pocket, a young man put his hand on my shoulder and walked me to the back. I was crying so hard, the young man looked like he was about to cry too. I think he wanted to let me go."

"What happened?"

"Well, in a little while a policeman came in, a real policeman in a uniform with a gun hanging on his hip. Now I was really getting scared. I think I was more scared of my daddy whipping me than the police. You see, my daddy didn't play when it came to stealing."

"You went to jail?"

"Well, no, but the good Lord sho' taught me a lesson."

"Then what happened?"

"The policeman was walking me down the street. I started begging and pleading more than ever. Snot was running down to my lip, huge teardrops were falling, and the policeman was quiet and kept walking. I was begging for my life. As we walked down the sidewalk, I knew we were getting closer and closer to my parents' car. All of a sudden, he stopped.

"He said, 'You ain't gonna do it again?'

"I said, 'I ain't gonna do it again.' I'm sure my heart almost stopped, waiting to see what he was going to do next."

Grandma Bee stared at the table.

"What did he do?" Kevin was eager to hear what had happened.

"Well, he looked at me for a moment and said I could go. Talk about feeling good—I felt like I had just been spared a life in Parchman Prison, wearing stripes with a ball around my ankle."

She laughed, then seriously said, "I thank God I got caught."

"You do?"

"Yes. Yes, I do. You see, if I hadn't gotten caught, I might have kept stealing, and stealing, and stealing. Now, if I had been stealing as a grown-up, I'm sure he would not have let me go."

"Wow, Grandma. You were a kid robber like Billy the Kid."

"Well, now, I wouldn't—well, I guess I was a kid thief," she admitted. "Now, back to what I was saying. In the days when Annie Mae was growing up, things were different. Yes, there were many who refused to live as slaves. Some escaped and moved to free states. Some tried to escape and were lynched. Some were tortured in ways you couldn't imagine. Folks did what they thought they had to do to stay alive. Some killed themselves and their children rather than let them live as slaves.

"Son, it wasn't easy for a grown man to have to call a boy Mister or have to walk off the sidewalk when a white person was coming. Or to feel like they had to laugh at a white person's joke when it wasn't funny. It wasn't easy for a mom to have to nurse the missus' baby first even while her baby was crying. Or to know when their children would be sold and they would never see them again. Some stuff was so bad, you're too young to hear about it."

"I know, Grandma. I saw some of 12 Years a Slave."

"What's that? A book?"

"No, a movie."

"Some got revenge in other ways. It wasn't the right thing to do, but some spat in the food they cooked. It didn't hurt no one, it just made them feel like they got a little revenge. Some sabotaged things when they thought they could get away with it."

She continued. "I remember my grandma telling me about a man named Mr. Festers. She said, and these are her exact words, not mines, he was 'a mean, low-down, dirty peckerwood.' He was mean to everyone: his wife and the slaves. You would think since he had a bad heart, he would be nicer, but he acted like he was mad at the whole world. He later lost his sight and he only got meaner. It got so bad his poor ole wife just left one day while he was asleep. She didn't take anything but the clothes on her back.

"Grandma said one time he thought one of the young men had stolen a two-pound bag of rice. He ordered them to tie him up and he beat him until his back was raw. They say Ole Man Festers later found the bag of rice on the floor of his buggy. Well, about a month later, that young man caught a rattlesnake while fishing. He decided to get even with Ole Man Festers.

"Later, one night the slave and one of his sisters who cooked and cleaned for Mr. Festers entered the house. The slave carried a stick and the snake in a croker sack. The sister stood watch at the door cause they knew there were two slaves on the plantation that would tell everything they knew. The slave tiptoed close to the bed and held the bag near Ole Man Festers's head while he slept. Then the slave hit the bag, causing the snake to rattle. Ole Man Festers started hollering and screaming hysterically. He was hollering, 'Help me, somebody! There's a snake in here!'"

Kevin was listening intently. He leaned on the table, waiting to hear more.

"Every time the snake would quiet down, the young man would hit the bag, causing the snake to rattle again. The sister was so tickled, she could hardly contain himself. The slave would hold the bag near Ole Man Festers's head sometimes and near his feet sometimes. After some time, they left.

"Early the next morning, the slave came and placed the dead snake in Mr. Festers's house shoe. Later, the sister came and cooked Festers's breakfast. He asked her to bring it to his room. He hadn't slept all night. The sister saw the snake in his shoe. She positioned the shoe so when he stepped out of bed he would step on the shoe. Well, you can imagine what happened, again."

She shook her head, laughing so hard her eyes were full of tears.

"They say he was never the same. He started treating the slaves nicer. Gave them more food rations. Why, he even made sure they had better clothes to wear in that hot sun. They no longer had to work on Sundays. He was a changed man."

She stopped smiling and got serious. "Now, that wasn't the right thing to do and it wasn't nice, especially since he had a bad heart. Poor ole man could have had a heart attack, but I bet it sure was a funny sight to see.

"Yes, there were a lot of brave men and women who wanted a better life, who wanted more for their children, who didn't sit around saying, 'Yessir, master," who knew they were not inferior, who knew they could do anything, and who wanted to be free at any cost. You see, greatness is in our DNA, and don't let no one tell you otherwise."

"Tell me some more, Grandma."

"Well, let me see—like Harriet Tubman."

"I already know everything about her. She drove a train underground."

"Are you kidding me? Where did you get that? No, no, no, she did not drive a train anywhere! As a child, she saw so much cruelty that she longed to be free. One day, when she learned that she was going to be separated from her family, she decided to escape. Two of her brothers left with her but got scared and turned back. She made it to Philadelphia and got herself a job as a cook, but she had no peace. She worried about her kinfolks back home. One day she met a son of an escaped slave and he told her about the Underground Railroad. She knew that God wanted her to help her people be free."

Grandma Bee continued. "Nobody knows exactly how many trips she made, but they say she made about twenty and helped free over three hundred people. That's why they called her Moses. She helped free her people. She also worked as a spy, scout, and cook for the Union Army."

Harriet pulled the trigger back on the pistol as she aimed it at one of the slaves' heads. "You ain't going nowhere! Too many people lives are at risk. They got a bounty on my head, dead or 'live. I ain't worried 'bout myself. I been beaten many times. I have scars that will go with me to my grave. Because I tried to stop a slaveowner from beating a slave, I got hit with an iron weight. To this day, I never know when I will just drop off to sleep. I never know if I will wake up and find a noose around my neck, but as long as the good Lord let me, I'm going to help my people be free."

The slave had been overheard talking. He was scared they would be caught and wanted to go back to the plantation. "Honest, I—I won't tell nobody nothin'," he stammered.

Harriet stared him straight in the eye. She didn't blink. "I hate to shoot you, but I can't have you tellin' all you know as soon as you get back. Your mouth would be running like a blabbering brook."

"Honest, no, I wouldn't! If you leave me here, right here, I won't—I won't say a thing."

With the gun aimed at his forehead. "If that's what you want, I will leave you here. A dead man can't tell nothin'."

The women whimpered and covered their faces. The men looked on in horror.

"No! No, please don't shoot. I'll go. I'll go."

She looked around at the others, making eye contact and holding it a moment with each one. "You be free or you die a slave."

A baby started to cry. She reached into her bag and placed a drug in his mouth to make him sleep.

She looked at the sky. "The sun is going down. We gotta get moving. Remember, if we get separated, follow the big star. It points north. If it's cloudy and you can't see the stars, 'member the moss grows on the north side of the tree trunk. Let's move out!"

"Man, Harriet was rough! Do you think she would have shot him for real?"

"Without a doubt! She might have been crying when she did it, but I'm convinced she would have pulled the trigger."

"You said she believed in the Lord. Slaves believed in the Lord?"

"Child, yes. They couldn't have made it without their faith. The master tried to stop them from worshipping, but they would slip out in the evening. They let the others know by singing 'Steal Away to Jesus.' Sometimes they carried quilts to cover themselves so they wouldn't be heard singing and praying. If anyone got happy or started shouting, they covered their mouth."

Kevin thought for a moment. "I know those mean old white folks didn't believe in God."

"Son, there are now, and there were then, a lot of decent white folks just as there were good black folks. Harriet Tubman didn't do all she did by herself. There were a lot of white people who hid the runaway slaves and gave them food and clothes along the way. Some white folks were called nigger lovers and even killed for helping slaves. You see your T-shirt?"

He looked down. "Yes."

"Does it only come in red?"

"No, it comes in all colors: red, white, blue, green—"

"And that's the way love and hate, good and evil comes—in all colors. Remember that."

He nodded his head and asked, "Why didn't they ask God to help them? Give them ideas of how to do stuff?"

"Boy, have you been listening to anything I've said?"

"I mean big ideas, like Alexander Graham Bell and Thomas Edison."

"Let me set you straight about something. A lot of those people that you read about didn't invent those things."

"They didn't?"

"Some did, but a lot of them didn't. You see, a slave couldn't get a patent or copyright, so because of that and the fact blacks couldn't read or write, the slave owners took advantage of them. The slave owners got the patents and the recognition . . . and, of course, the money."

"Wow!"

"But a lot did get their recognition. My favorite is Mr. George Washington Carver!"

"Oh, I know about him. He gave us sweet potato pie and peanut butter, right?"

"Wrong. Where you get that foolishness from? No, that's not right! He did things greater than pies and peanut butter."

Sitting on a stool in his lab, George reaches into his smock pocket for his pencil before remembering it was on his ear. Tired and worried, he scribbled on his notepad.

Across the room, Booker T. Washington looked on. "I just don't know, George. The farmers appreciate you teaching them about crop rotation, but now the advice you gave them about planting peanuts isn't going so well. Farmers planted the peanuts like you said, but they aren't selling so well. We have too many. I hear some of the farmers are really upset. I understand that the minerals in the soil have been depleted because of years and years of cotton crops. Thanks to you, the land has been replenished, but George, the peanuts aren't selling." He scratched his head. "I'm afraid a lot of farmers are going to lose their farms." He looked over at George, who was busy at work, before he slowly walked out the door.

George looked up toward Heaven and prayed, "Lord, ever since I was a young man, I rise early and talk with you. I trust you and I will continue to trust you."

The next morning George rose early, as was his custom. As he walked, he talked to the Lord. "Lord, I know peanuts is the solution, but please tell me why it's valuable so the crop rotation can be implemented."

George sensed the Lord saying, "Separate the peanut into water, fats, oils, gums, resins, sugars, starches, and amino acids. Then recombine these under my laws of compatibility, temperature, and pressure. Then you will know why I made peanuts."

In less than two weeks, George had discovered more than three hundred uses for peanuts, including cosmetics, dyes, paints, medicine, and food products. He also discovered over a hundred uses for sweet potatoes.

Later, Booker T. Washington was sitting in George's office. He shook his head. "I got to tell you, George, the next time you tell me something, I won't doubt you."

"Wow. We didn't learn all of that in school."

"Oh, and you won't, but the half hasn't been told. George was truly a gifted man. Even as a child, he was interested in nature and had a green thumb. People were always asking him to nurse their plants back to health even before he could barely read. He used his knowledge mostly to help poor farmers in the South, especially sharecroppers. He invented a horse-drawn classroom and laboratory so he could demonstrate and explain out in the fields. It was called the Jessup Wagon. Many don't know it, but George played the piano and accordion and they say he could really sing."

Kevin piped up. "When I was in fifth grade, during Black History month, my friends and I were in the cafeteria. One of the Asian boys thought we had taken his milk off his tray. He said all of us ought to go back to Africa, where we came from."

"What did you do?"

"I told him to go back to China."

"Is that all you did?" Grandma Bee had heard from his mom that Kevin wasn't one to let stuff slide.

"Well, I said he ought to go back to China with his old squinch-eyed self. All the kids started laughing, and then he started crying. Both of us got in trouble and had to go to the office."

She looked at him. "You know which part of that was wrong to say, right?"

He nodded.

"I had a lady tell me the same thing when I was in line getting ready to vote for President Kennedy."

"What did you do, Grandma Bee?"

She tried to circumvent the question. "What I did was no better than what you did."

He persisted. "What did you do?"

"Well, it wasn't nice. I shouldn't've gotten so mad."

"What did you do?" he continued to ask.

"Well, I said, 'Sure, and I'll drop you off in Ireland to dig potatoes on my way to Africa.' People started clapping for me and she turned as red as a—as an apple."

"Ooooooh, Grandma Bee!"

"No, no, it wasn't right . . . but it sure felt good. I don't understand how other people who came from another country can feel that we should go back to our native country. Everyone in America came from another part of the world, including the Native Americans."

"Even the Native Americans?" he asked, surprised.

"Son, even the Native Americans. Civilization didn't start in North America and what do you think discover means?"

"To find something or to learn something new."

"Listen to me closely, now. I have never seen the Grand Canyon. Now, if I go to the Grand Canyon tomorrow, can I say I discovered it?"

"No. Lots of people have been to the Grand Canyon already."

"There were lots of Indians here in America when Christopher Columbus came also."

His eyes lit up, and as he leaned in, she knew he understood.

"Grandma Bee, what happened after the Civil War? Weren't the slaves free then?"

"Child, no! Well, near the end of the Civil War, in 1865, General Sherman led tens of thousands of freed slaves across Georgia to the Carolinas. He signed an order promising them forty acres of land and a mule, but when the war ended three months later, President Jackson ordered all the land to be returned to its previous owners. So they had a choice: either they could sign a one-year labor contract to work on the farms, or they would be arrested for vagrancy, for wandering on other people's land.

The slaves knew how to farm cotton and white people needed workers for the fields, so that's when sharecropping came into play. Black families could work the land and give the owners a portion for rent. Often the landowner would furnish the seeds and equipment. But no matter how hard they worked, somehow at harvest time the families always owed and the debt had to be carried over to the next year. Even though most of them couldn't read or write, they knew they were being cheated, but what could they do? They knew they wouldn't win in the white man's court. The way I see it was just slavery by a new name.

"This period was called Reconstruction. President Lincoln started it right before the war ended. Unfortunately he was killed a week after the Civil War ended. The first Reconstruction Act was passed, allowing black men the right to vote. The whites weren't happy, to say the least, about slaves being set free. They weren't about losing all of that free labor.

It was around this time when the white supremacist group, the Ku Klux Klan, started terrorizing the black communities. They started out with just six members who wanted to restore white supremacy in the South. Some, they say, wore robes to appear as ghosts to scare the superstitious blacks. They wore those pointed hats and masks to hide their identity because many of them were sheriffs, politicians, doctors, lawyers, well-known people of the community, sometimes even preachers. They killed black political leaders and heads of churches. They also burned homes with families inside, shot up churches, and drove many blacks off their farms. Some folks said a couple of our former presidents were KKK members."

She continued. "White folks had something called a Black Code. It kept our people from conducting business, from owning land. We couldn't buy or lease, but then they turned around and criminalized the men who were not working. In Mississippi, if you weren't able to take care of your children, the law allowed the state to take the children and give them to the former slaveowner. They were always making up some new law black people had broken. When we couldn't pay the high fines, they hired us out to the highest bidder. The purpose was to keep slavery alive.

"White folks in charge always tried to make sure we wouldn't succeed. I read that in the 1920s, they spent about thirty-six dollars to make sure each white child got a good school education, but only spent around five dollars for each black child.

"They made up laws to keep blacks from voting. We had to pay a poll tax for two years before the election. Blacks couldn't afford it. Then they had the literacy test. We had to read a section of the state constitution and explain it to the county clerk. Of course, the clerk was always white. The clerk would decide if we were literate. Of the voting-age black men, 60 percent couldn't read and the clerk would select complicated passages to interpret. For the white people, the clerk would pick simple sentences to explain. Mississippi was one of the worst. Their law had a grandfather clause. You could only vote if your grandfather before the Civil War could vote. Naturally, that ruled out most of the blacks. Black voting went from 90 percent to 6 percent by the late 1890s."

"Man, Grandma Bee. Were you living during slavery?"

"Do I look like I'm over a hundred years old, boy?"

Kevin opened his mouth.

"Watch your mouth, now. Watch your mouth."

Kevin closed his mouth, then asked, "I mean, how—you've learned so much. You didn't even go to high school."

"Child, I dropped out of school; I didn't drop out of life! As long as you're living, you should be learning, growing. That's what's wrong. Too many people feel the only place to learn is in some kind of school. On the farm, you learn how to cook, sew, garden, do carpentry. You don't need to go to school to learn skills. And Kevin, especially your generation."

"You mean I don't have to go to school?" he grinned.

"Yes, yes you do. Look-a here. How do you play dominos?"

He grabbed his phone. "I'll show you." He pulled up a tutorial on YouTube.

"Uh-huh. Oh, what's the first line in the Constitution?"

"Hold up, I'll get it." He stopped and smiled. "I know what you're doing."

She smiled back. "You see, you were able to find the answers, and you didn't find them at school. Why? Because nowadays, you have a school in your hand, and in your case, the school is in your hand all the time. I want you to start researching your history. The more you know about the greatest of your people, the more confidence you have. You walk different. You talk different. You live different. You won't settle for mediocrity. You'll realize that greatness is in you also.

"As a people, we've always been able to achieve a lot. It's not that we can't. The sad thing is there are always others who try to keep us down by any means necessary. You see, grandbaby, in the early 1920s, blacks had over a hundred black towns across America. One black neighborhood that stood out was in Tulsa, Oklahoma, called Greenwood. It was a booming oil town. Some called it Black Wall Street. The neighborhood had over thirty grocery stores and meat markets. They had their own banks, photography studios, dry cleaners, dental offices, jewelry stores, hotels, restaurants, and furriers, a public library, two newspapers, and real estate agencies. They had everything they needed. There were several black millionaires in that town, and several even owned their own airplanes. A dollar would stay in the community for nearly a year. Whites were jealous, especially poor whites who thought they were superior. They started targeting black veterans and black businesses. They saw blacks as becoming too powerful, too wealthy. They were looking for an excuse to destroy and riot in black neighborhoods.

"One day a white lady said a young black man assaulted her in the elevator. White vigilantes looted the stores and set them on fire. An eyewitness said he saw about twelve airplanes dropping flaming jars of turpentine on buildings, setting them on fire. Blacks were machine-gunned down in the street. In less than two days, the black neighborhood was totally wiped out. They say over a thousand homes were destroyed and over three hundred people, mostly blacks, died. The governor called in the National Guard and declared martial law, but by that time everything was destroyed."

She shook her head.

"What?" Kevin asked.

"Hours after the attack, they dropped the charges against him. They said he either stumbled into her or stepped on her foot. Of course, you won't learn about this in your history book. Think about it: if our ancestors could accomplish great things with the odds against them, how much more can we do with greater opportunities in 2020? It depends on how bad we want something.

"So, grandbaby, it's not that we don't have the wealth to do great things in our community. One of the problems, not the only one of course, but one of the problems we face is spending our dollars in our neighborhood. We run to their neighborhoods to shop, we run to their neighborhoods to dine. We are going to have to start shopping in our neighborhoods. We are going to have to start pooling our money together and opening great restaurants and clothing stores. After all, we are some of the best cooks in the world. I know many black women who can sew anything they see without a pattern. We can do it. We've done it before. We just have to come together.

"For too long, we let their mindset rub off on us. We looked down on our own people with darker skin and treated light-skinned people better. We started talking about good hair and bad hair. The good Lord made all of our hair, so all hair must be good. We spend a fortune on weave and false eyelashes, trying to make ourselves beautiful when we are beautiful just the way we are."

"Grandma Bee, don't you wear weave?" he asked. He had seen her brushing her long hair one morning.

"No, child. This is what God gave me and I take care of it. My mama didn't fry my hair when I was growing up. She said if the Lord wanted me to have straight hair, He would have given it to me. So I never put chemicals in my hair. I just wash it and keep it oiled."

She continued. "Let me tell you about another person. This is my favorite."

"You said that the last time."

"Well, I guess I have a lot of favorites. I just got to tell you about a guy named John Brown."

Kevin jumped up and slid across the floor on one leg. "Papa gotta brand new bag!" He did a split. "Ouch," he said as he slowly rose and limped back to the table, rubbing his leg.

"No, that's James Brown."

"Aw, yeah. You're right."

"Did you hurt yourself?"

"No, I'm okay."

Noticing the clock on the wall, she said, "Oh, my. It's getting late, but I want you to know how far people will go to get something if they want it bad enough, so let me tell you about a black man named John Brown."

"James, I need your help. You're a free man and, like you, I'm determined to be free. It was bad enough that I couldn't live in the house with my own wife because she's on another plantation. But then, I'm here in Virginia and seeing her, our

children, and our baby in her belly that I will never see. To see them in chains being sold to someone in North Carolina, well, it's more than a man can take. I watched, standing helpless, not able to do anything for my family. Lord, Lord, Lord. So, I've made up my mind, I'm gonna be free. I need you to help me. I got a little money saved up. I'm willing to part with it all to stand on free soil one day."

John continued. "I believe the good Lord has given me the gumption and a plan, but I need help to carry it out. It may sound crazy, but I'm gonna ship myself to Philadelphia."

James stood dumbfounded. He wasn't sure if it could be done, but he was willing to help him try. He knew a white man who sympathized with the slave and he agreed to help, for a profit of course. John paid him eighty-six dollars.

Finally, one day in the spring of 1849, John got into a box that was three feet tall, two and a half feet wide, and two feet deep. The box was lined with a woolen cloth. He had only a bladder of water and a few biscuits. It had a hole cut in the side for air and the words THIS SIDE UP written in big letters, but several times during the trip the box was turned upside down. On one occasion while it was upside down, it felt like his eyeballs would burst out of their sockets as the blood rushed to his head. Fortunately for him, two men turned it right side up to sit on.

Finally, after twenty-seven hours, by wagon, railroad, steamboat, and ferry, he reached his destination. When they opened the box, he quoted the book of Psalms: "I waited patiently on the Lord and He heard my prayer."

"I would have been scared to trust that white man. I would have been scared he would run off with my money."

"Sometimes you just have to trust people. My Papa use to say you have to trust your gut."

"I know he was uncomfortable in that box. Shucks, I be squeezed all up when Mrs. Field down the street take all of us to school in her Volkswagen, and that's only for a few minutes."

"Well, John said it like this—let me see if I can get it right. Ah, he said, 'If you have never been deprived of your liberty, as I was, you cannot realize the power of that hope of freedom, which was to me indeed, an anchor to the soul both sure and steadfast.'"

"Wow, some slaves did become great in America!"

"Wrong, wrong, wrong! Son, we were not slaves brought to America. We were great warriors, inventors, doctors, musicians, priests, farmers, goldsmiths, and such who were enslaved and then brought to America. We were and are a great people and we helped to make this nation great. During the 1800s, cotton was king in the South, and just who do you think was planting, chopping, and picking it from sunup to sundown?

She paused. "Don't your mom take you to Sunday School?"

"Sometimes. Sometimes we oversleep."

"Have you ever heard about the three Hebrew boys, Jewish boys?'

"Yes. My teacher calls them Shadrach, Meshach, and a bad—"

She raised her hand, stopping him. "I know, I know, I've heard that before! Well, when the Babylonians captured

56   GREATNESS — IT'S IN YOU!

them, they were great people. As a matter of fact, the poor, the weak, and the sick they left behind. The good book said the king wanted people of the royal family. He wanted the strongest and the smartest people. He wanted people who could quickly learn new skills.

"So, you see, the white folks knew how to indoctrinate a people the same way. Many of them were wicked to the bones, but they had seen how it was done before. Like the Israelites, we were not slaves. We became enslaved. "

Grandma Bee sat up straight. "We were a proud people! And just like back in the Bible days, one of the first things the slave owners did was change our names. They wanted to separate us from our rich heritage, from our identity, from our native land, from our faith. They packed us in ships like sardines with barely enough room to move a muscle. No ventilation. Just enough food to keep us alive. Conditions so bad, many of us jumped overboard and some tried to starve ourselves to death and were literally force-fed. When we got deathly sick or died from malaria, yellow fever, or smallpox, they threw us overboard like an old shoe. They say so many bodies were thrown overboard that the sharks would follow the slave ships.

"Many fought back. The most famous revolt was on the Amistad. A group of fifty-three Africans were kidnapped and were being taken to Cuba and sold into the Spanish slave trade. The slaves revolted and took over the ship. They were forcing the captain to take them back to Africa. They used the sun to navigate during the day, but at night the captain would change the course and head toward Cuba. They ended up in New York. The slaves were placed in custody while they sorted out the whole thing. The case ended up going all the way to the Supreme Court, which ruled in their favor. The court said they were illegally transported and held as slaves and they had a right to rebel in self-defense. At the end of the day, the slaves were set free and thirty-five of them sailed back to Africa.

"Grandbaby, the problem is that for too long, the only images we saw of our people portrayed us as barbaric, lazy, inferior, good for nothing but cheap labor, shuffling around the master's mansion. The first slaves knew they came from greatness and they fought back. Nat Turner, Denmark Vesey, and many others led revolts. Baby, when you know that greatness is in you, you don't just settle for anything. Remember, the only people who can be kept down are the ones who feel inferior, the ones who don't know their history. The funny thing is, we may not know our history, but believe me, other folks do. They learned how to read and write, and they kept records. Even the cruel stuff done to our people, they know. It's unbelievable, but they took pictures of bodies hanging from trees and made them into postcards to send to their families and friends. They even took body parts of the hung person to keep as souvenirs. Believe me, they know. They know."

"It's sad that much of our history has been lost to us, but still, we know enough to know we come from greatness. I read that one of the wealthiest people who ever lived was an African king named Mansa Musa. He was a Muslim. Once he went on a pilgrimage to Mecca with over sixty thousand people in his entourage. It was like a city moving through the desert. They say all of the people were dressed in gold brocade and the finest Persian silk. He had hundreds of camels carrying hundreds of pounds of gold."

"Wow! He was richer than Jay-Z and Beyoncé put together."

"Child, he was richer than Jay-Z, Beyoncé, Oprah, Bill Gates, and Warren Buffet all put together!"

Kevin's eyes got wider as she called each name.

"Africa is the richest continent on the face of the earth."

"Wow, Grandma Bee, I didn't know that."

"Look at the Jewish people today in America. Because they know their history, they are some of the wealthiest people on earth. The owner of the Chicago Bulls and the White Sox, the Facebook guy, Bill Gates—they know who they are. They can trace their roots back thousands of years and when you have been taught from birth about your rich history, you walk differently, you think differently, and you live differently. I believe that's why our history has not been taught in the public schools. Oh, they stuck three or four black people's names in the textbooks, but our contributions to making this country one of the greatest countries on earth have been mostly omitted.

"The laws in America, for hundreds of years, have been designed to keep us down, to separate us from our heritage, but I got a strong feeling that times are changing."

"Why you say that, Grandma?"

"Because we are realizing that even though others have tried to keep us down, we played right into their hands. For the most part, we're not challenging our children to live up to their full potential. Yes, we know they are smart. We see that all the time, how they can create something great out of broken things. Many of our young men can build computers.

The way they come up with great rap songs, dances. How they can run a street business.

"But, grandbaby, we need to push them more. Well, maybe not push, but nudge them more when it comes to learning. It doesn't have to be their heads in a book, either. Learning, exploring, and thinking outside of the box instead of having their eyes glued to a video or the TV. Education is key. We have to stop stressing the need to get a job and start training them to think about owning a business, and we have to start when they're young. You have to be taught more about the Bible than just Moses parting the Red Sea and David killing Goliath. You must be taught that God said He gives you the power to get wealth. Remember what I told you about George Washington Carver? He asked God for answers and God gave them to him. God is just waiting on us to ask for new ideas, new inventions.

"It's sad that, unlike a lot of people, we can only trace our history back three or four generations. We can't go all the way back to our great-great-great-grandfathers who were wealthy kings in Africa, and because of that partly, we are where we are today. Shucks, I can only go back to Annie Mae.

"But, baby, just remember: just because bits and pieces of the puzzle are missing, there is no reason for us not to excel. Believe me, we have enough to know what the puzzle is, know enough about those who came before us to ignite a fire in our bellies that—that can't be extinguished and we won't settle for—"

"Mediocracy. You mean mediocracy!" he added proudly.

Grandma Bee was impressed. "Yes, that's the word I want to use."

GREATNESS — IT'S IN YOU!

"My teacher uses it all the time."

"Think about it this way." She took a moment and composed her thoughts. "If I was competing against MJ and Kobe was competing against MJ, who do you think MJ would be more worried about, me or Kobe?"

"Grandma, you can't—"

"Answer the question, child!"

"Kobe, because he is as great as MJ or greater."

"You see? You don't have to suppress or try to hold a person down if you don't feel that he has greatness in him. You just let him be."

"Wow, you know a lot of stuff. I thought you didn't—"

"Watch your mouth."

"I mean, I thought—uh—uh, people who were really old, I mean, grown people didn't know a lot of stuff."

"What made you think that?"

"Well, because you all don't know how to work computers and iPads. Mama didn't know how to set the TV—"

"Yes, you're right. Now, watch this." She grabbed one of his sheets of paper and wrote in cursive, "My grandson is as lazy as all get out."

"What does this say?" she asked, holding it up. He looked befuddled. She laid the paper down. "What time is it?"

He reached for his phone.

She was faster. "No, read that clock on the wall."

He looked up at the wall. He squinched his eyes, bit his lip, and frowned, but none of those exercises gave him a clue. "I don't know."

"Okay, one last thing: how much is 345 plus 345 plus 345?"

He reached for his pencil.

She was faster. "No pencil."

With a look of defeat, he said, "Grandma, I guess don't none of us know everything, huh?"

"None of us, Kevin."

Grandma Bee got up and felt the pot to see if it was cool. She lifted the lid and breathed in the aroma of garlic and onions. A smell of fall permeated the kitchen.

Kevin, with his eyes on her, quietly folded the sheet of paper she had written on and shoved it into his pocket.

She glanced out the kitchen window and noticed that, for the third time this month, the traffic light on the corner was out. "That's reminding me of another great problem solver, Garrett Morgan. Have you ever heard of him?"

"Yes, he invented the traffic light," said Kevin.

"Well, he improved the one they already had and he invented other things. You see, the one they had only had a red and a green light for stop and go. He invented the three-way light. It had a stop and a go light, but it also had a third light to stop traffic from all directions and allow people to cross the street. But before that, in 1914 he invented a kind of hood that would allow people to breathe in the midst of gases, smokes and pollutants. Because Morgan was black, many white folks didn't want to buy it even though it worked and saved lives. However, Garrett was smart. He found and hired a white actor to pretend to be the inventor. He also posed as the inventor's assistant and was the one going into places with smoke and gases to show how well it worked. All of a sudden, people loved the mask. Fire departments and rescue workers started buying them like hotcakes.

"About two years later in Cleveland, Ohio, some men were trying to find a fresh water supply under Lake Erie when something went terribly wrong. They hit a pocket of gas underground and it caused a big explosion. Some of the men got trapped underground. Morgan and his brother were able to go into the tunnel wearing the masks he had invented and were able to save two men and remove the bodies of others."

"Wow. I bet they call that day Garrett Morgan Day like they do now when people are heroes," said Kevin.

"You would think, but I'm afraid you're wrong. On the contrary, because they were black, the city didn't even recognize them for the successful mission. On top of that, they refused to buy masks that could save lives simply because the inventor was a Negro. I'm sure that must have hurt a little, but Morgan kept right on going. The mask proved to be very popular. Over fifty cities adopted it, including New York City. He also had several other inventions."

She pulled her glasses off and cleaned them on the tail of her apron. "People talk about making America great, but we did it already. If it's messed up, it isn't because of us. Every great invention in America, we played a role in, from electricity to the telephone, a man on the moon, yes, we played a major role in it."

"I know about the black ladies who helped put the first man on the moon. My teacher told us about Dorothy Vaughan, Katherine Johnson, and Mary Jackson, but I thought Thomas Edison invented the light bulb?"

"Well, the history books said he did, but what your history books didn't tell you is that a black man named Latimer Lewis improved his bulb."

"What about the telephone? We helped invent that, too?"

"Well, let's put it this way: Lewis Latimer also worked closely with Alexander Graham Bell."

She continued. "We all know cotton was what helped America become a great nation. A slave named Ned invented a double plow scraper. It could scrape the ground on both sides of the cotton row simultaneously, saving time and labor. Some people even say that it was a black man who invented the cotton gin and not Eli Whitney."

"I've learned a lot about history today. This is like watching a movie. It's not boring at all, Grandma Bee. Thanks."

"Your mom won't be back for a couple more days. In the meantime, we're going to learn more history. You see, you need to learn not only about George Washington, but George Washington Carver. Not just Christopher Columbus, but Crispus Attucks. Not just Benjamin Franklin, but Benjamin Banneker. Not just Betsy Ross, but Bessie Coleman. Kevin, hear me clearly: greatness—it's in you. Oh, I forgot to tell you about one of—"

"I know—one of your favorites."

"Just listen, child. A slave named Thomas Fuller was snatched from his native land when he was fourteen. He was considered illiterate because he couldn't read and write, but, boy, could he work with numbers. He could solve complex math problems in his head. I'm talking about problems you need a calculator to solve, like 234 times 45. I mean like one time they asked him how many seconds are in a year. In less than two minutes, he gave them the answer. They worked the problem out with paper and a pencil. Guess what? He was right.

"A lot of wealthy white folks wanted to buy him, but his slave owners wouldn't sell him. You see, they couldn't read and write either, but they had enough sense to know that Thomas was an asset to them. They said that Thomas could tell you how any shingles you needed for a new roof or how much corn to plant in a field or how many poles you needed for a pasture. Even when he was in his seventies, they were still coming to him like they did Solomon in the Bible. People came from miles around to test his math skills and see if he was as good as they said . . . and he was."

"Wow!"

"Oh, I have to tell you about one more. This one is my fa—"

Kevin looked up as if to ask, "Another favorite?"

"Well, let's just say this a good one. Do you like spy movies?"

"Yes, I saw Spy Kids.

"Then you gonna love this one."

Chapter 4

Jefferson Davis was sitting at the dining room table with two other men in uniform. They were strategizing about the war, discussing troops, ammunition, and food supplies. Unbeknownst to them, Mary was moving slowly, memorizing every tiny detail that was said as she served their lunch.

"Mary, bring me those papers from the table in my study upstairs."

"Yessir, master," she replied as she filled their wineglasses.

She hurried up the stairs. She took her time, carefully memorizing everything she read.

After about five minutes, noticing she hadn't returned, one soldier said, "Those are important papers, Davis. They should be kept under lock and key."

Davis replied with a laugh, "Mary is the only one in the house. What do you think she's gonna do? Read 'em and give the info to Grant?" They all roared with laughter.

Mary walked back into the room and handed him an old newspaper. "Like I said, I don't think we have to worry about Mary," he said as he held up the newspaper. They laughed in agreement. He stood. "I'll get them. Be right back."

Mary continued to clear the dining room table, moving slowly to obtain more information. As Davis walked back into the dining room, there was a knock at the door.

Mary turned to the grandfather clock. "It's 8:00 a.m., master. It's Mr. Niven bringing yo' favorite sweets this morning, just like he said."

Mr. Davis and the other men were so busy looking over the papers spread out on the table, they didn't hear her.

Mr. Niven was a baker who often made deliveries to the Davis home, but he was also a member of the spy ring. Mary walked outside to his buggy.

As they wrapped up the meeting, Davis walked the men to the door. At a distance, they observed Mr. Niven giving Mary a large basket filled with freshly baked pastries and bread. What they didn't see was the wealth of information she was giving him.

As she slowly made her way past them, she overheard one say, "She's so slow, it's a good thing we aren't depending on her to win this war."

They roared with laughter. Mary smiled, too.

After lunch, Mary cleared the table, did the dishes, and rushed to do the laundry. Mr. Davis noticed she only had two pieces on the clothesline: a white shirt and a pair of pants.

"Didn't you wash the laundry yesterday?"

"Yessir."

He shrugged his shoulders and mounted his horse. What he didn't know was that a white shirt beside a pair of upside-down pants meant General Hill was moving troops to the west.

"Wow—a spy just like James Bond!" Kevin's eyes were wide with pride.

"Yep. Mary was born a slave, but when her master died, his daughter Mary Van Lew freed the slaves she inherited. She saw how smart Mary was, so she sent her to a colored school. She even went to Liberia in Africa as a missionary for a few years, but came back to help fight for freedom here.

"Ms. Van Lew got Mary a job in the Confederate White House, where Jefferson Davis lived. She took advantage of the little respect they had for slaves and even exaggerated it, playing like she was slow and mentally challenged, but all the time she was gathering information. She would act like she was blundering around the house. She might as well have been a piece of furniture since they paid her no mind. All the while, she was eavesdropping and writing down valuable information to pass on. They said sometimes she sewed messages into women's dresses. They just couldn't figure out how the information was getting out. She was the last one they suspected. But, eventually, somehow they realized it had to be her and she had to flee."

"Wow. What happened to her?"

"She later founded a school to teach black people. She taught a day school, a night school, and a Sunday school.

"And it wasn't just Mary. We had many more during the Civil War. The last ones they suspected were the slaves. After all, most slaves couldn't read and write."

"Now, that's smart!" Kevin noted and raised his hand. Grandma Bee high-fived him.

"Son, in this country blacks have fought for everything we've gotten. No, I don't mean physically fighting, or stealing or looting. That's wrong all day long, and two wrongs have never made a right. But there are other ways we can fight.

We fight with our votes, our voices, and Lord knows we can fight with our money. People may not respect your black or brown skin, but they will respect your green dollars and your silver coins."

He shook his head.

"In the '50s, a young boy not much older than you was murdered. His name was Emmitt Till. He lived right here in Chicago with his mom. That summer he was visiting some of his relatives in Money, Mississippi. One day, they say, after a long day in the field picking cotton, he and some more boys went to the store to buy some refreshments. The store owner's wife, a white lady, said he grabbed her waist and said something offensive to her.

"Anyway, a few days later, around three in the morning, some men went to Emmitt's uncle's house and kidnapped him. They took him to the riverbank, made him take off his clothes, beat him nearly to death, gouged out one of his eyes, and dragged his body to the bank of the river, then shot him in the head. If that wasn't bad enough, they tied him with barbed wire to a metal fan and threw him in the Tallahatchie River.

"Three days later the authorities pulled his body from the river. It was unrecognizable. It didn't look like a human. His mom had the body shipped back to Chicago. God bless her soul. I don't know how she was able to do it, but she insisted on an open casket funeral. Thousands of people saw his water-soaked, bloated-beyond-recognition body lying in the casket. She wanted the whole world to see what racism looks like in America."

Kevin was so quiet. He had heard of Emmitt Till, but he knew none of the details other than that white people had killed him.

Grandma Bee was very quiet. One look at her face and Kevin knew her memory had taken her back all of those years.

He waited patiently, but was eager to learn more.

She continued. "I remember going to work right after that, early one Saturday morning. I walked into the house and I could tell immediately that Mr. and Mrs. Benson had been arguing. They weren't talking to each other, so I knew it was serious. I went in the bedrooms and started making the beds.

"All of a sudden, I heard the front door slam. About that time, Mrs. Benson came into the room where I was. I knew something was up because she was mighty quiet. I didn't say anything. I thought maybe they were getting a divorce. She said they had a bad fight with her in-laws about Emmitt Till. She said that anyone who could do that to another human being, especially a child, was not human." Grandma Bee paused. "And then she said anyone who thought it was okay was just as bad, and she walked out. I knew at that moment I wouldn't be returning to work on Monday."

Kevin was stunned. He had never heard that story before. "That's too sad."

"No, child. What was too sad was the fact that the lady confessed years later that she made it up. The only thing that child had done was whistle at her. The two men were acquitted by an all-white-men jury. They knew they couldn't be tried again, so they confessed to killing him a few months later. They lived their lives in freedom."

Kevin pretend not to notice as she wiped the tear from her eye. "Grandma, why they hate us so much? How can they think they are better than us?"

"Child, I don't think they do."

With a look of confusion, Kevin asked, "Huh?"

"You see, they couldn't possibly believe the slaves were too nasty to eat out the same plate that they ate out of, cause, after all, we cooked the food, washed the plate, and put the food on it. And they couldn't think we came from monkeys, cause when we had babies we nursed their babies along with our own. They couldn't possibly think we were nasty cause their menfolks slept with our womenfolks and had babies just like they did with their wives."

She continued. "You know who Thomas Jefferson was, right?"

"Yeah, one of our presidents."

"Well, do you know who Sally Hemings was?"

"The first lady?"

"Well," she chuckled, "I guess in a way she was, but not really. She was a slave who lived with him and he was the father of six of her children. You see, son, if people don't want to accept a truth, they can fool themselves into believing a lie. It's called denial, but that's not our problem—it's theirs.

"People are just like flowers; they come in many colors. One race is no better or worse than the rest. We all came from the same two people, Adam and Eve. The Bible tells me everything that God made is good, and that includes you and me. So, don't linger on the past. Know it, but live in the present, right now, and be excited about your future."

She sat up straight and continued. "I know they taught you about Rosa Parks, right?"

"Yeah, a little."

"Well, a few months after they killed Emmitt Till, it was right after Thanksgiving, Mrs. Parks was coming home from work after a long day of standing on her feet. She got on the bus and went back to the colored section like the law required. Well, more and more white people got on the bus, so the bus driver wanted her and a few other blacks to give their seats to whites who were standing up. The other blacks gave up their seats, but she said no. The driver was furious. He called and had her arrested. Later that night she was released on bail.

"A few days later, the black community, who made up 75 percent of the bus ridership, were encouraged to not ride the bus for a day. So 90 percent stayed off the buses. Many carpooled, some rode in black-operated cabs, and a whole lot of people walked to work and school. Some they say walked over fifteen miles a day. It was so successful, they decided to boycott even longer. Some of the white folks got mad. They bombed Dr. King's house and some churches. They cancelled the insurance for some of the black cabs. They arrested people for boycotting. It lasted 381 days, but black people won the right to sit wherever they wanted to sit on the bus.

"Kevin, it's like those teacakes. If you want something better, you have to never take no for an answer. You have to keep moving forward, don't settle, keep pushing and pushing and pushing. Nothing worth having is going to be easy. You have to work at it, child."

She pushed back from the table, walked over to the cabinet, and pulled out two cookie sheet pans. "Come on, it's getting late. Let me help you with your essay, and then we can bake those teacakes."

Kevin hesitated.

"Now what?" she asked.

"I think I want to do the essay on my own."

She looked deep into his eyes, and she knew. "All right."

He grabbed his book, paper, and pencil and headed down the hall. As he approached the threshold of his door, he stopped, turned, and went into the bathroom instead. He placed his paper and pencil inside his book and laid it on the edge of the tub.

He held the sink as he stared into the mirror. Eleven-year-old Kevin stared back at him. He took a deep breath and closed his eyes as he replayed the stories, one after another, that Grandma Bee had taught him. Minutes later he opened his eyes. Staring back at him from the mirror was an African warrior. He was bronzed, strong, and fierce, wearing a necklace of stones and teeth. A kente cloth was draped over his bare right shoulder and a spear was in his right hand. He stared back and nodded. Kevin nodded, too.

Later, Kevin shared all the stories with his best friend Shawn, who wanted to hear more. He came over every day after school.

But Grandma Bee enjoyed it even more than the boys. She fixed them snacks and shared many interesting stories about slavery, Jim Crow, and the Civil Rights Movement. The boys always listened intently.

Kevin shared all the stories with his mom when she returned. She was happy to hear that he had enjoyed the time with his great grandmother and impressed with how much he had learned.

Epilogue

Two months later, back in Mississippi, the rain tapped softly on the awning with a steady rhythm as Grandma Bee poured her morning coffee. She carefully measured one tablespoon of creamer and a teaspoon of sugar, snatched a paper towel off the roll, and headed to the living room. She felt her age this morning and looked it, too, she thought as she passed the mirror on the hall wall. The twinkle in her eyes was missing, along with the joy in her heart.

She stumbled on the rug and spilled coffee down the front of her duster. She placed her mug on the end table, sat down, and dabbed the stain with her paper towel, then pulled the ottoman near and lifted her legs to rest. Grandma Bee had lived alone since her husband died eighteen years earlier, but she hadn't felt lonely in years. Now her home felt empty, and she felt alone.

It wasn't a mystery! The fact was, she was missing Kevin. The first couple of days had been challenging, but the rest of the visit, she'd felt useful as she shared stories of their rich heritage. They'd even found time to share a few knock-knock jokes at the dinner table.

Grandma Bee smiled and picked up her pencil and crossword puzzle. She rarely finished one. Somehow there were always one or two clues she couldn't answer. From now on, she determined, things would be different. She would finish each one no matter how long it took.

She chuckled as she looked at the first clue going down: "to grip firmly." She had no idea. The first clue going across was a seven-letter word for battered veggies. Easy. Tempura.

"Ah-ha!" She went back to the first word, wrote tenacity, and smiled.

The phone rang.

"Hello?"

"Happy birthday, Grandma Bee! I'm sorry I didn't get your card in the mail on time, but you should get it tomorrow." It was Bridgette.

"Is it my birthday again already? Look like I just celebrated one."

"I also want to thank you again for keeping Kevin on such short notice since his father was on a cruise."

"Child, you have thanked me ten times. No need to thank me—that's what families do, look out for each other."

"I don't know what you did during those two weeks, but my child has changed."

"Oh?"

"No, I mean in a good way. He seems to be more focused on his schoolwork. In the last week, he's brought home two A's and a B. It's unbelievable! I mean, not that he can't do it, but that he is doing it. I think he's into drawing or something. He hides it from me, but he spends a lot of time writing or drawing. Maybe it's a birthday surprise. All I know is I love the new-and-improved Kevin."

They both laughed. Grandma Bee said, "I think sometimes we just need a little reminding that if we're not succeeding the way we want to, maybe, just maybe, it's because we don't want it bad enough."

"Hmm . . . if we're not, maybe . . . That's good. I'm going to remember that one. Well, I gotta run, on my way to work.

"Don't forget, you should get your card tomorrow or the next day, and remember we would love for you to come and stay a month or so. Gotta run! Love you! Bye."

"Bye. Love you more!"

Grandma Bee hung up the phone and heard yip-yip, yip-yip, yip-yip.

"Thanks, Yorkie, for the notice." Yorkie was the neighbor's Shih Tzu. She sat at the open window and let everyone know the moment the carrier parked on the block.

"Thanks, Yorkie."

Thump. The mail was placed in the box.

"A four-letter word, second letter is I . . . list in a program . . . uhh—oh, a bill."

She penciled in the letters: B-I-L-L.

"Speaking of bills," she mumbled. She laid her book down and went to get the mail. She flipped through the stack of envelopes. "Light bill, phone bill, bank statement, something from a credit card, no thank you, not interested—uh, what's this? Such a beautiful yellow envelope. Huh. Nice cursive handwriting, but no return address."

A bright yellow or pink envelope could mean only one thing: birthday or Mother's Day. Unless you were sick and it was a get-well card. She threw the stack of mail on the coffee table and ripped open the yellow envelope.

She could hardly believe it. The card was from Kevin.

"Grandma Bee, thank you for teaching me that greatness is in me. Love, Kevin." It was all in cursive. At the bottom it read, "P.S. I am not as lazy as all get out anymore and I would like to spend part of my Christmas break with you. I want to learn more about our history. Love, Kevin."

Two small hearts were drawn at the bottom.

She smiled as she held the card close to her chest. It warmed her heart. As she passed the window, it was still raining. Everything looked the same, yet everything had changed.

Two months before, she was just your typical eighty-nine-year-old grandma who loved the Lord and enjoyed going to church on Sunday and working on her puzzles through the week. Other than talking with her neighbor Maria across the fence as they sat on their back porches in the evenings, most of her days were spent alone and she was content, but something had changed. She had changed.

Kevin had changed.

She smiled and picked up the phone.

"Hello, I'd like to make a reservation for the first of May."

"To Chicago."

"Ah, make that a one-way, please."